INTERACTIVE LESSON PLANNERS

Progressive Maths

Unit 1: Counting

Julie MacLure

Published by Julie MacLure, with the assistance of:

Lumphanan Press
Roddenbrae
Lumphanan
Aberdeenshire
AB31 4RN

http://www.lumphananpress.co.uk

ISBN: 978-0-9955323-0-4

Interactive Learning Psychological Services Limited

TEACHER NOTE • COUNTING

Numbers to 10:
recognition of digit and word

Outcome: Number, money and measurement

Strand: Add and subtract

Target: add and subtract – mentally for numbers 0 to 10.

AIMS

The pupils should know the numbers up to 10 and be able to recognise a number as a digit and in words.

OBJECTIVES

To teach the relationship between number, digit and written word.

INTRODUCTION

Practice materials such as blocks should be used to count first. Pupils should be encouraged to count out loud.

COUNTING

Colour 1

Copy and complete

one

o

Colour 2

Copy and complete

two

t

Colour 3

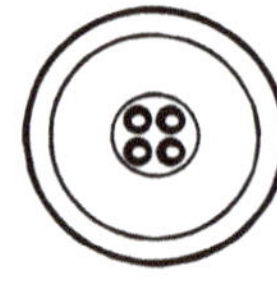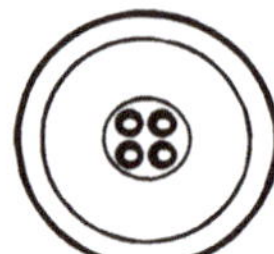

Copy and complete

three

t

COUNTING

Colour 4

write four

Colour 5

write five

Colour 6

write six

COUNTING

Colour 7

write seven

....

Colour 8

write eight

....

Colour 9

write nine

....

COUNTING

Colour one

write one, 1

Colour two

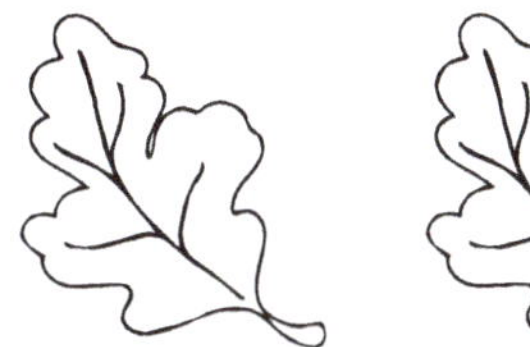

write two, 2

Colour three

write three, 3

COUNTING

Colour four

write four, 4

Colour five

write five, 5

Colour six

write six, 6

COUNTING

Draw and colour seven	write seven, 7
Draw and colour eight	write eight, 8
Draw and colour nine	write nine, 9

MATCHING

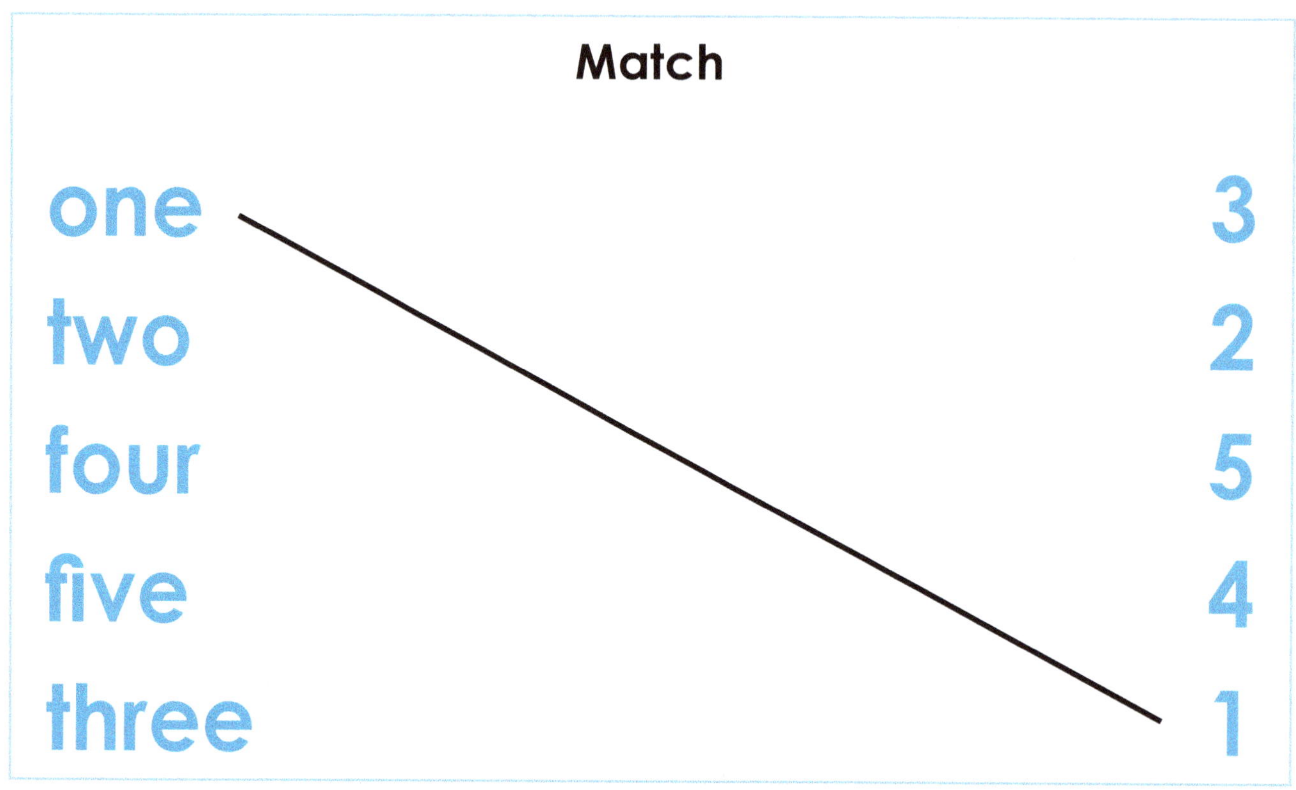

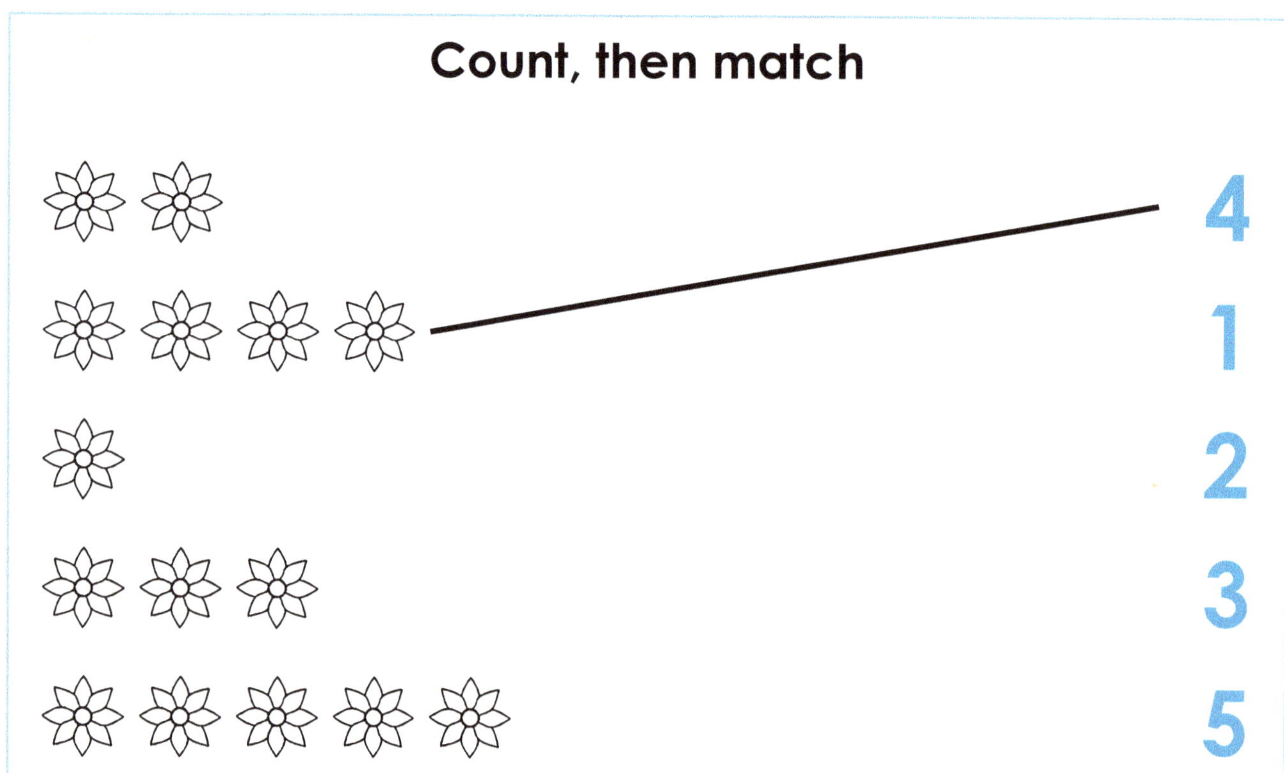

MATCHING

Count, then match

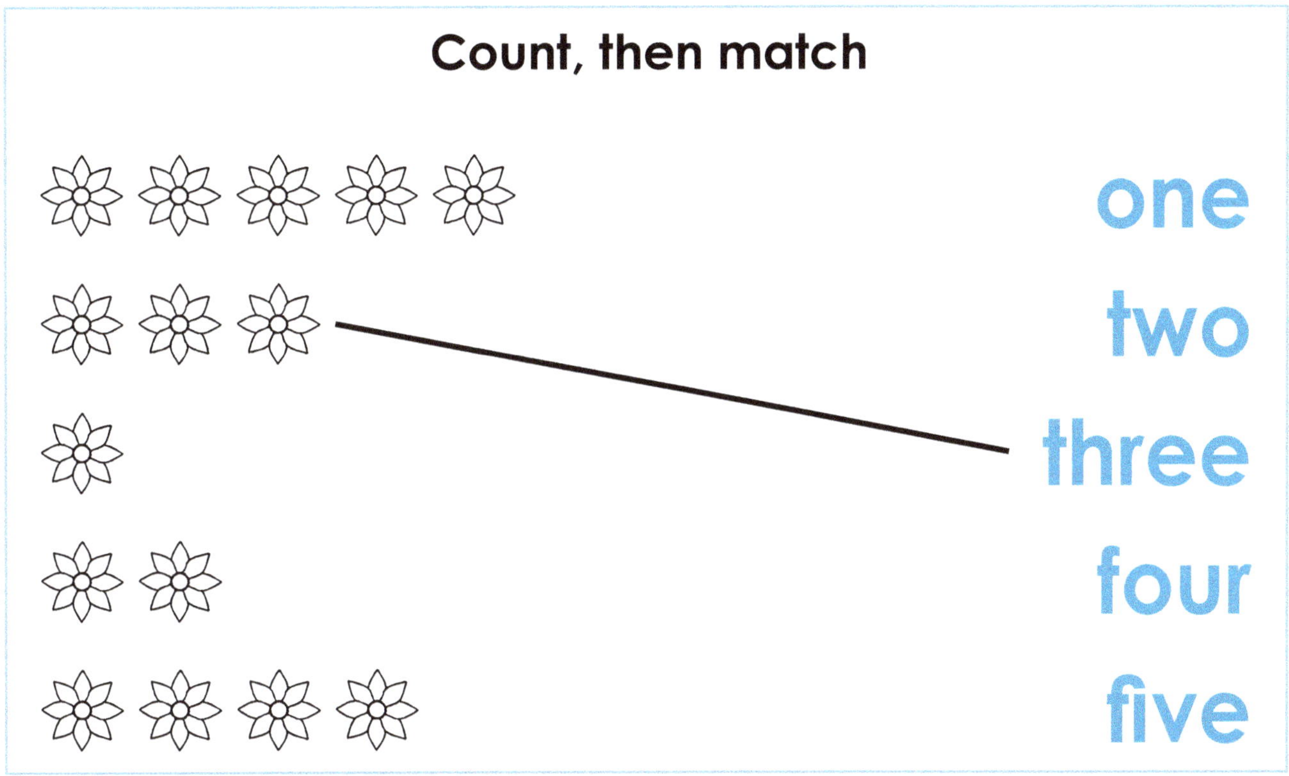

one

two

three

four

five

Match

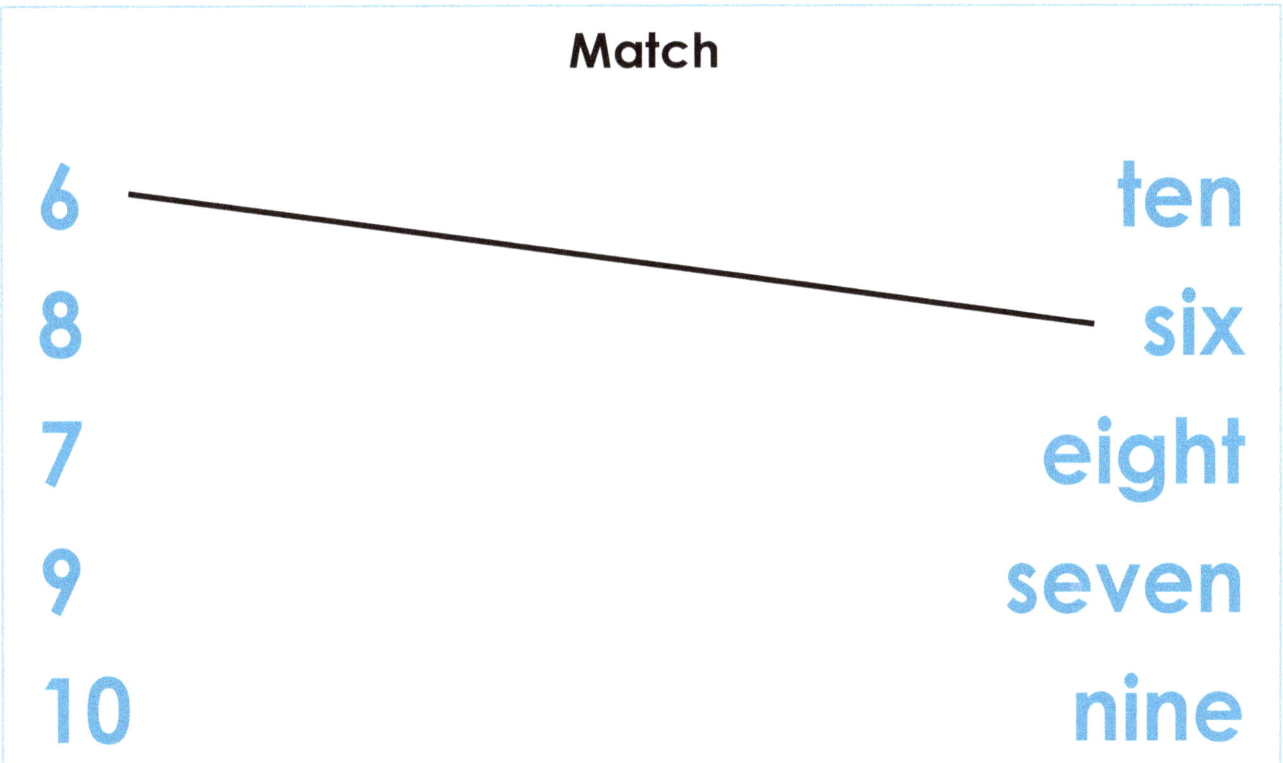

6   ten

8   six

7   eight

9   seven

10   nine

MATCHING

Count, then match

9

10

8

7

6

Count, then match

6

7

8

9

10

MATCHING

Put the numbers in order

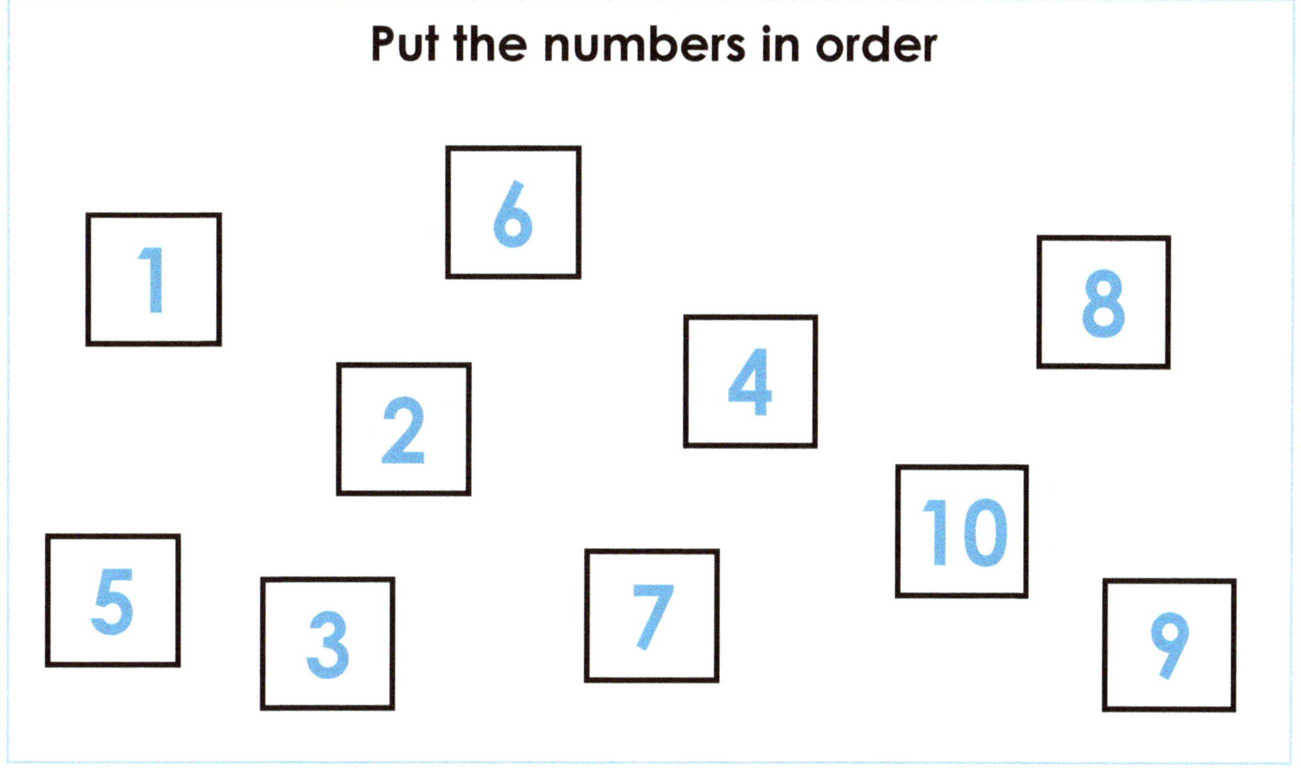

JOIN THE DOTS FROM 0 TO 6 AND COLOUR

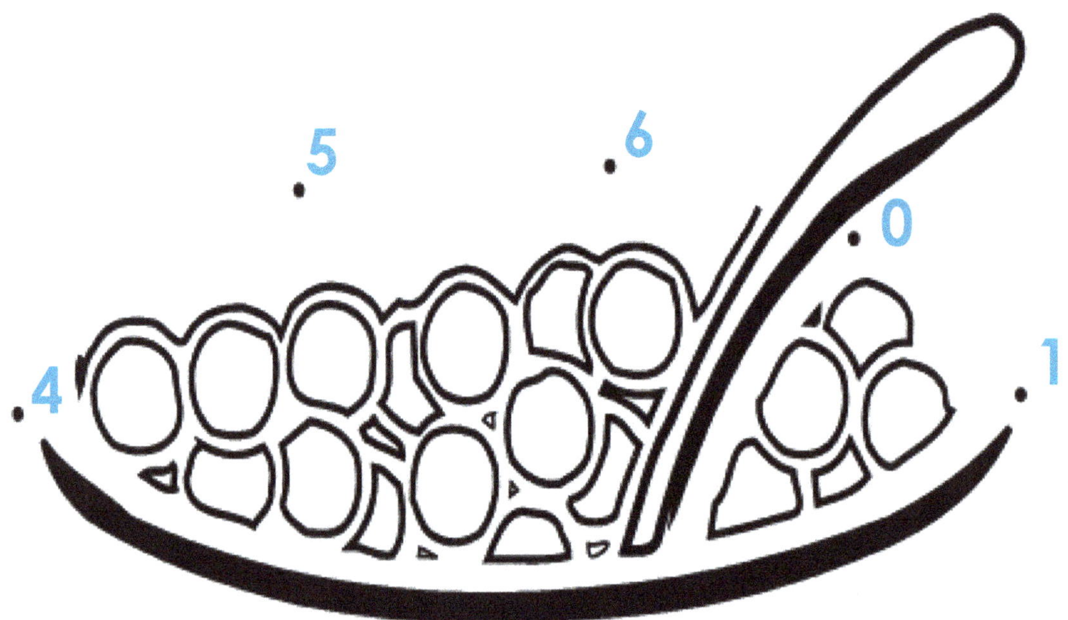

JOIN THE DOTS FROM 0 TO 8 AND COLOUR

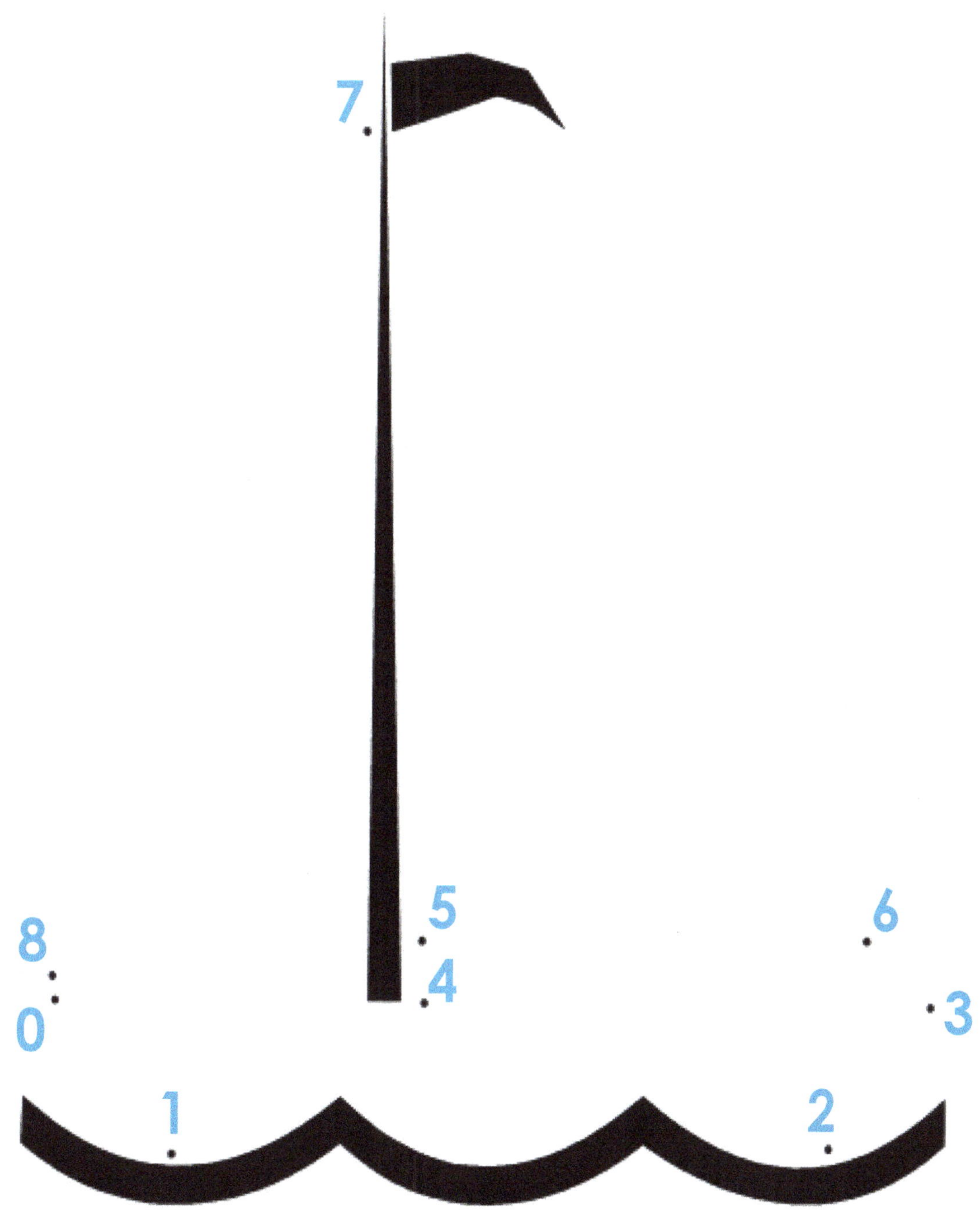

NOTES

PROBLEM SOLVING

For this activity you will need, a paper fastener and a scissors.

Cut around the clock face after colouring it in. Cut out the clock hands. Then attach to the centre of the clock with a paper fastener.

Group Activity

Play guess the time. Set the hands to an on the hour time then ask your group if they know the answer. The group then write the time down. See how many times you get right. Each take a turn at setting a time.

www.ingramcontent.com/pod-product-compliance
Lightning Source LLC
Chambersburg PA
CBHW041352050726
47599CB00016B/1865